FRANCIS FRITH'S

NEWQUAY TO ST IVES

PHOTOGRAPHIC MEMORIES

PETER STANIER was born in Liskeard and has written several books and papers on Cornish subjects, in particular mining and quarrying, as well as Francis Frith's *Cornwall Living Memories, Victorian and Edwardian Cornwall, Churches of East Cornwall, Photographic Memories of Britain: Cornwall, St Austell* and *St Austell Bay*. He lives with his family in Shaftesbury, Dorset, where he is a lecturer and writer on archaeology, industrial archaeology and landscapes.

FRANCIS FRITH'S
PHOTOGRAPHIC MEMORIES

NEWQUAY TO ST IVES

PHOTOGRAPHIC MEMORIES

PETER STANIER

First published in the United Kingdom in 2004 by
Frith Book Company Ltd

Paperback Edition 2004
ISBN 1-85937-817-X

British Library Cataloguing in Publication Data

Francis Frith's Newquay to St Ives - Photographic Memories
Peter Stanier
ISBN 1-85937-817-X

Frith Book Company Ltd
Frith's Barn, Teffont,
Salisbury, Wiltshire SP3 5QP
Tel: +44 (0) 1722 716 376
Email: info@francisfrith.co.uk
www.francisfrith.co.uk

Printed and bound in Great Britain

Front Cover: **ST IVES,** *The Harbour c1955* S22038
Frontispiece: **HAYLE,** *Towans and the Beach 1927* 80084

The colour-tinting is for illustrative purposes only, and is not intended to be historically accurate

AS WITH ANY HISTORICAL DATABASE THE FRITH ARCHIVE IS CONSTANTLY BEING CORRECTED AND IMPROVED AND THE PUBLISHERS WOULD WELCOME INFORMATION ON OMISSIONS OR INACCURACIES

CONTENTS

FRANCIS FRITH
VICTORIAN PIONEER

FRANCIS FRITH, founder of the world-famous photographic archive, was a complex and multi-talented man. A devout Quaker and a highly successful Victorian businessman, he was philosophical by nature and pioneering in outlook.

By 1855 he had already established a wholesale grocery business in Liverpool, and sold it for the astonishing sum of £200,000, which is the equivalent today of over £15,000,000. Now a very rich man, he was able to indulge his passion for travel. As a child he had pored over travel books written by early explorers, and his fancy and imagination had been stirred by family holidays to the sublime mountain regions of Wales and Scotland. 'What lands of spirit-stirring and enriching scenes and places!' he had written. He was to return to these scenes of grandeur in later years to 'recapture the thousands of vivid and tender memories', but with a different purpose. Now in his thirties, and captivated by the new science of photography, Frith set out on a series of pioneering journeys up the Nile and to the Near East that occupied him from 1856 until 1860.

INTRIGUE AND EXPLORATION

These far-flung journeys were packed with intrigue and adventure. In his life story, written when he was sixty-three, Frith tells of being held captive by bandits, and of fighting 'an awful midnight battle to the very point of surrender with a deadly pack of hungry, wild dogs'. Wearing flowing Arab costume, Frith arrived at Akaba by camel sixty years before Lawrence of Arabia, where he encountered 'desert princes and rival sheikhs, blazing with jewel-hilted swords'.

He was the first photographer to venture beyond the sixth cataract of the Nile. Africa was still the mysterious 'Dark Continent', and Stanley and Livingstone's historic meeting was a decade into the future. The conditions for picture taking confound belief. He laboured for hours in his wicker dark-room in the sweltering heat of the desert, while the volatile chemicals fizzed dangerously in their trays. Back in London he exhibited his photographs and was 'rapturously cheered' by members of the Royal Society. His reputation as a photographer was made overnight.

VENTURE OF A LIFE-TIME

Characteristically, Frith quickly spotted the opportunity to create a new business as a specialist publisher of photographs. He lived in an era of immense and sometimes violent change.

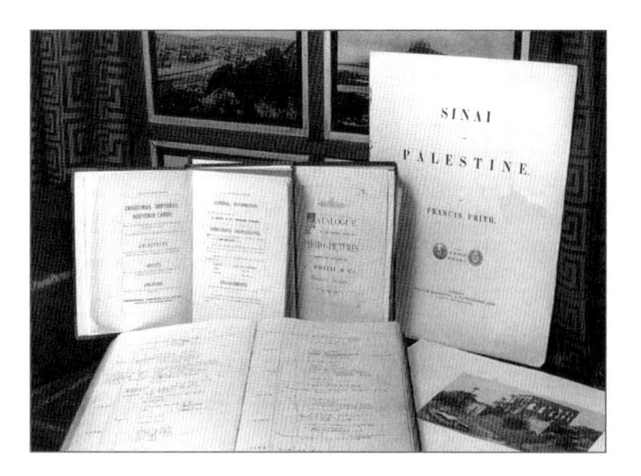

For the poor in the early part of Victoria's reign work was exhausting and the hours long, and people had precious little free time to enjoy themselves. Most had no transport other than a cart or gig at their disposal, and rarely travelled far beyond the boundaries of their own town or village. However, by the 1870s the railways had threaded their way across the country, and Bank Holidays and half-day Saturdays had been made obligatory by Act of Parliament. All of a sudden the working man and his family were able to enjoy days out and see a little more of the world.

With typical business acumen, Francis Frith foresaw that these new tourists would enjoy having souvenirs to commemorate their days out. In 1860 he married Mary Ann Rosling and set out on a new career: his aim was to photograph every city, town and village in Britain. For the next thirty years he travelled the country by train and by pony and trap, producing fine photographs of seaside resorts and beauty spots that were keenly bought by millions of Victorians. These prints were painstakingly pasted into family albums and pored over during the dark nights of winter, rekindling precious memories of summer excursions.

THE RISE OF FRITH & CO

Frith's studio was soon supplying retail shops all over the country. To meet the demand he gathered about him a small team of photographers, and published the work of independent artist-photographers of the calibre of Roger Fenton and Francis Bedford. In order to gain some understanding of the scale of Frith's business one only has to look at the catalogue issued by Frith & Co in 1886: it runs to some 670 pages, listing not only many thousands of views of the British Isles but also many photographs of most European countries, and China, Japan, the USA and Canada - note the sample page shown on page 9 from the hand-written Frith & Co ledgers recording the pictures. By 1890 Frith had created the greatest specialist photographic publishing company in the world, with over 2,000 sales outlets - more than the combined number that Boots and WH Smith have today! The picture on the next page shows the Frith & Co display board at Ingleton in the Yorkshire Dales (left of window). Beautifully constructed with a mahogany frame and gilt inserts, it could display up to a dozen local scenes.

POSTCARD BONANZA

The ever-popular holiday postcard we know today took many years to develop. In 1870 the Post Office issued the first plain cards, with a pre-printed stamp on one face. In 1894 they allowed other publishers' cards to be sent through the mail with an attached adhesive halfpenny stamp. Demand grew rapidly, and in 1895 a new size of postcard was permitted called the court card, but there was little room for illustration. In 1899, a year after Frith's death, a new card measuring 5.5 x 3.5 inches became the standard format, but it was not until 1902 that the divided back came into being, so that the address and message could be on one face and a full-size illustration on the other. Frith & Co were in the vanguard of postcard development: Frith's sons Eustace and Cyril continued their father's monumental task, expanding the number of views offered to the public and recording more and more places in Britain, as the

5	" Queens College, View from the garden	+
6	" St Catherine's College	+
7	" Senate House & Library	+
8	"	+
9	" Gerrard Hostel Bridge	+ + + +
30	" Geological Museum	+
1	" Addenbrooke's Hospital	+
2	" St Mary's Church	+
3	" Fitzwilliam Museum, Pitt Press &c	+
4	"	+
5	Buxton, The Crescent	+
6	" The Colonnade	+
7	" Public Gardens	+
8	"	+
9	Haddon Hall, View from the Terrace	+
40	Miller's Dale	+

coasts and countryside were opened up to mass travel.

Francis Frith had died in 1898 at his villa in Cannes, his great project still growing. The archive he created continued in business for another seventy years. By 1970 it contained over a third of a million pictures showing 7,000 British towns and villages.

FRANCIS FRITH'S LEGACY

Frith's legacy to us today is of immense significance and value, for the magnificent archive of evocative photographs he created provides a unique record of change in the cities, towns and villages throughout Britain over a century and more. Frith and his fellow studio photographers revisited locations many times down the years to update their views, compiling for us an enthralling and colourful pageant of British life and character.

We are fortunate that Frith was dedicated to recording the minutiae of everyday life. For it is this sheer wealth of visual data, the painstaking chronicle of changes in dress, transport, street layouts, buildings, housing, engineering and landscape that captivates us so much today. His remarkable images offer us a powerful link with the past and with the lives of our ancestors.

THE VALUE OF THE ARCHIVE TODAY

Computers have now made it possible for Frith's many thousands of images to be accessed almost instantly. Frith's images are increasingly used as visual resources, by social historians, by researchers into genealogy and ancestry, by architects and town planners, and by teachers involved in local history projects.

In addition, the archive offers every one of us an opportunity to examine the places where we and our families have lived and worked down the years. Highly successful in Frith's own era, the archive is now, a century and more on, entering a new phase of popularity. Historians consider the Francis Frith Collection to be of prime national importance. It is the only archive of its kind remaining in private ownership. Francis Frith's archive is now housed in an historic timber barn in the beautiful village of Teffont in Wiltshire. Its founder would not recognize the archive office as it is today. In place of the many thousands of dusty boxes containing glass plate negatives and an all-pervading odour of photographic chemicals, there are now ranks of computer screens. He would be amazed to watch his images travelling round the world at unimaginable speeds through internet lines.

The archive's future is both bright and exciting. Francis Frith, with his unshakeable belief in making photographs available to the greatest number of people, would undoubtedly approve of what is being done today with his lifetime's work. His photographs depicting our shared past are now bringing pleasure and enlightenment to millions around the world a century and more after his death.

NEWQUAY TO ST IVES
AN INTRODUCTION

THIS SELECTION of photographs includes images taken from 1890 until the 1960s along 30 miles of the north Cornish coast between the two very different 'honey pot' resorts of Newquay and St Ives. There are high cliffs of shales and slates, rugged headlands, and long beaches of fine golden sands exposed at low tide. Two great areas of blown sand form high dunes at Penhale and Hayle Towans. The few harbours are small and difficult of access, but full of character. All this has drawn tourists to the district since the second half of the 19th century.

This landscape is steeped in history. At Penhale Sands we see the ruined oratory of St Piran, who is the patron saint of Cornish tinners. A similar chapel discovered at Gwithian is no longer visible, but Phillack church near Hayle seems to be on an early site. This whole area was a landing place for the Celtic saints who crossed over the seas from Ireland and Wales - legend says that St Piran came from Ireland on a mill-stone. Medieval churches can be seen at St Columb Minor, Crantock, Cubert, Gwithian, Phillack, Lelant and St Ives, with 19th-century examples at St Ives and Perranporth. The Elizabethan manor of Trerice is a real surprise, and makes a pleasant contrast to the nearby crowded bustle of Newquay.

HAYLE, *Towans and the Paddling Pool 1925* 78626

Fishing was traditionally important along the coast. It is best seen at St Ives harbour, but pilchard boats were launched from beaches elsewhere, including Porthminster and Perranporth. Many Cornish ports thrived during the days of metal mining in the 19th century, and Newquay's harbour was improved to serve the mines. Portreath was built solely for the mining trade, and Hayle was an industrial port with foundries and mineral wharves.

The mining industry is ever present, with distant engine houses breaking the skyline at Perranporth, or ruined landscapes around St Agnes, Porthtowan, Carbis Bay and St Ives. Railways served the mines, and also especially the tourist trade in its early years. The development of tourism is seen through the pleasures of the beaches, while large hotels make their appearance at Newquay, Perranporth and St Ives - even golfers are catered for.

Our coastal tour starts at the major resort of Newquay, which features grand hotels and golden beaches. The Atlantic Hotel dominates the town and the beaches from the Beacon. Built in 1893, it was described at the time as a 'handsome building of stone' set in 5 acres of grounds, which 'from its elevated position commands an uninterrupted ocean view from every window: the large coffee room, drawing, reading, billiard and smoking rooms are noble apartments; the main hall is very spacious and contains a fine fire-proof staircase reaching to every floor.' There were over 100 apartments.

Other Newquay hotels are the Great Western and the Hotel Victoria; the former is now greatly altered in appearance since a major refurbishment in 1931. The Headland Hotel was opened in June 1900, overlooking Fistral Beach from Towan Head. Rivalling the Atlantic, it is a fine example of a late Victorian hotel built to impress. It was designed by the noted Cornish architect Sylvanus Trevail, who made much use of decorative terracotta for the exterior. While the Atlantic Hotel has now lost its chimneys, the Headland retains much of its original extravagant appearance. In contrast, we see the National Children's Home out on what was a remoter headland at Pentire. This later became a hotel, and is now surrounded by housing developments.

The origins of Newquay's harbour lie in a 'new quay' built in the late 16th century. It was developed in the 1830s by Richard Lomax, and then after 1838 by the industrialist Joseph Treffry for the export of minerals and china clay. Pilchard fishing, although important, came second to the mineral trade. Railway branches served the china clay district and the copper and iron mines to the south, and in 1849 a tramway was run down an incline through a tunnel into the harbour area. Further improvements came in the 1870s when the Cornwall Minerals Railway built a wooden bridge out to a stone pier in the middle of the harbour for exporting iron ore and china clay. At the same time a rail connection was made with Par, at last giving Newquay direct access from the Great Western Railway, and therefore also giving a boost to the town's potential as a tourist resort. The railway into Newquay crossed the Trenance valley on a viaduct. The first viaduct had stone piers carrying a timber trestle top, which was later replaced by iron girders (as seen in this book); it was finally rebuilt with stone arches in 1939. The harbour tramway was closed in 1926, but its course through the town has been preserved as a footway. The last trading ship called in 1922, and the harbour has since been given over to fishing and pleasure boats. A lifeboat was stationed at Newquay from 1860 until 1945, with a brief closure in 1934-40. The lifeboat house on the neck of Towan Head was opened in 1899 - it had one of the steepest launching slipways in England.

The beaches have always been the greatest attraction for visitors to Newquay. The photographs show the Towan, Great Western and Tolcarne beaches beneath the cliffs along which the town's hotels and guest houses developed. The sands are busy with holidaymakers at different times between 1901 and 1925, with beach tents and even bathing machines in attendance. They contrast with the wilder Fistral Beach, which is backed by dunes and golf links.

The Gannel estuary is a real physical barrier between Newquay and the quieter village of Crantock. It is sandy at low tide, where a crossing can be made on foot, but it becomes a long arm of the sea when the tide is in; there was once a proposal to turn it into a permanent lake behind a dam. Crantock's old village stocks are seen preserved behind the church. They once stood inside the tower, where their last occupant was William Tinney, who robbed a Cubert widow with violence in 1817. He managed to escape the stocks, and then climbed inside the tower, cut the bell rope and used it to lower himself down outside where he made his getaway, never to be seen again. Crantock church is unusual, with its chancel taller than the nave.

The church at Cubert is of interest because it has a spire, which is rare in Cornwall. It stands on high ground between Crantock and the great dunes of Penhale Sands. In the centre of this landscape of sand hills, partly colonised by grasses, is the 6th-century oratory dedicated to St Piran. Long lost under the blown sands, it was excavated in 1835 by William Michell: he found a shrine for the saint's relics in the tiny building, with several skeletons buried under the floor. The exposed ruin suffered from souvenir hunters and the incursion of sand, so it was enclosed within a concrete building in the 1930s. More recently, the whole site has been deliberately reburied.

Perranporth was a fishing and mining hamlet long before the tourists came. The place is beginning to develop in the early photographs, and one shows the railway branch which ran from the main line at Chacewater to Newquay. There is evidence of tin, copper and lead mines dating back to the 16th century in the cliffs around Droskyn Point, and the distant engine houses of the Penhale Mine appear in another view. In the neighbourhood, Harmony Cottage near Mithian was the birthplace of John Opie (1761-1807), the 'Cornish Wonder', who became a famous portrait painter in London.

Traces of mining are very much more in evidence around St Agnes and Porthtowan. St Agnes had a very exposed shipping pier for the mines down at Trevaunance Cove, but only the rubble remains after it was washed away. Now the beach in the cove attracts bathers and surfers. The intriguing little harbour at Portreath exported thousands of tons of copper ore to South Wales in the 19th century. It is seen in decline when a few steamships still visited, bringing coal. The narrow entrance between a pier and a dangerous cliff was hazardous; but the risk was justified, because Portreath was the closest harbour to the copper and tin mines around Redruth and Camborne.

Down towards Hayle and St Ives Bay, the

Godrevy lighthouse is a reminder of the dangers found along the north Cornish coast. It was erected in 1859 after a long period of wrecks on the offshore reef known as the Stones. The deciding wreck was the 700-ton steamship 'Nile', which had been lost with its crew and passengers five years before. The white tower on its island is visible from across the bay at St Ives, and it was the inspiration for Virginia Woolf's book *To the Lighthouse*.

The Towans, dunes lying behind the 3-mile beach between Gwithian and the Hayle estuary, match those at Penhale. Early signs of tourism are in evidence, with tents, caravans and chalets among the grassy dunes, while holidaymakers enjoy the sandy beach below. Phillack is a village separate from Hayle; carved stones at the church indicate a very early Christian site here, perhaps with connections with the Irish saints. Hayle itself grew up in the 18th and 19th centuries as an industrial town and port, with smelters (the name Copperhouse still survives) and foundries serving the tin and copper mines, while its long wharves shipped off copper ores and imported coal.

On the far side of the estuary, Lelant has a fine church next to the golf links, where the West Cornwall Golf Club of 1889 is the oldest in the county - not all holidays are spent on the beach. The little branch railway to St Ives is seen beside the saltings at Lelant, and again as it passes Carbis Bay, a resort that has changed much since the first photographs. The beach, overlooked by the Carbis Bay Hotel, provides safe bathing.

St Ives is seen in the days when fishing was the mainstay of the port. Photographs taken on different dates show changes around the town and harbour, such as the building of the Porthminster Bay Hotel or the harbour wall of the Wharf, while the fishing vessels alter in design and decline in numbers. We see the railway when the station was a terminus which gave travellers a true sense of arrival. Its long platform and station buildings have, alas, become a car park, and trains now run into a featureless little stopping place. The old parish church stands just the same, although changes are seen in its immediate surroundings. Its mellow granite stones contrast with the harsher design of the Victorian church of St John. Mining took place around the town, as we can see from an engine house at Pedn Olva between the harbour and Porthminster Beach, and the ruins of the little-known Carrick Du mine at Man's Head in a view across Porthmeor Beach to the Island.

Our tour ends on a hill overlooking St Ives and the Bay, with the memorial to John Knill: he intended it to be his tomb, but he was buried in London, where he died in 1811. He left a legacy so that he is remembered in a curious ceremony held every five years on St James' Day - it involves 10 girls in white, two widows, a fiddler, the parson, a customs officer and the mayor. There are far-reaching views of Cornwall from this high spot on a clear day, and the coast is visible all the way to Newquay and beyond.

NEWQUAY

NEWQUAY
Trevelgue Head and Watergate Beach 1899 43177

'Rugged beauty' might be the words to describe this view: we are looking down over the tide-covered sands of Lusty Glaze from the Barrowfields on the very edge of Newquay. Trevelgue Head is also known as Porth Island, and is separated by a deep ravine crossed by a footbridge. The long sandy beach of Watergate Bay is in the far distance.

NEWQUAY
The Great Western Hotel 1887 20253

The hotel was built on Tolcarne Point in 1875 close to the railway station - the 1870s were the pioneering days of tourism. A path led down to the sands of Great Western Beach below. This comfortable hotel is now hardly recognisable after enlargements and stylish alterations in 1931.The rough gravel surface of Cliff Road in the foreground is now the principal road into Newquay.

NEWQUAY, *The Hotel Victoria 1900* 45856

The newly completed Hotel Victoria in East Street is much larger than the Great Western Hotel, and it is also convenient for the railway station. The grand design, hardly changed today, reflects the growing confidence of Newquay as a resort in late Victorian times.

NEWQUAY
Cliff Road 1918 68675

A few horse carriages and carts, a bicycle and one distant motor car are the only vehicles in the street during the last year of the Great War. The nearest carriage waits outside the Great Western Hotel, and behind it a sign directs pedestrians to the cliffs and beach. The small gardens fronting the terraced houses on the right have long since been swept away for shops and a wider pavement.

HIGHWAYS
COACHES
START HERE
TO THE
SALOON
WHOLE DAY TOU
GOLD FLAKE
Library

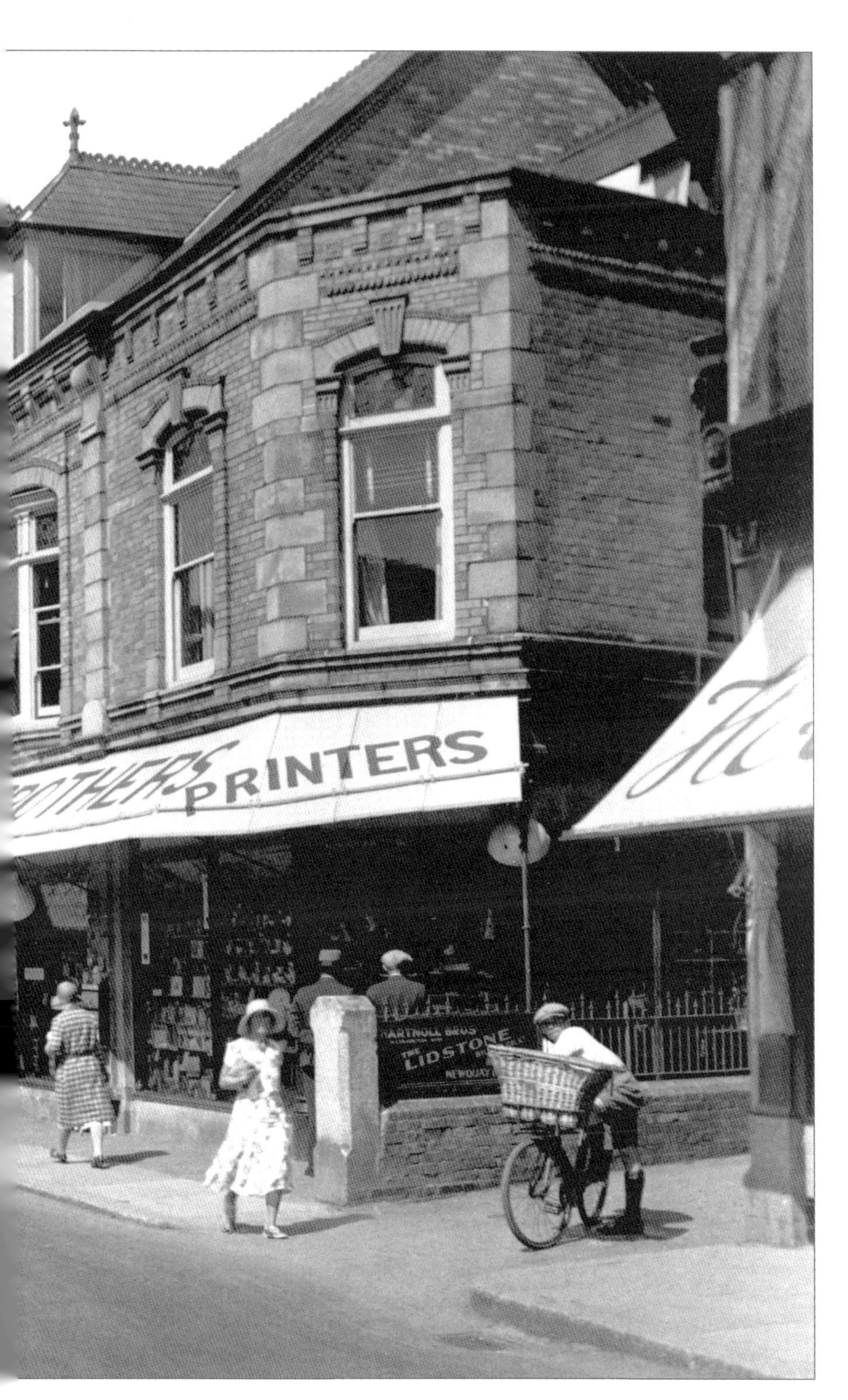

NEWQUAY
Bank Street 1930 84395

This quiet scene in the heart of the shopping district lacks the bustle of modern Newquay. A delivery boy rests with his bicycle between rounds on the right, while down the street a policeman looks out for traffic to direct. Hartnoll Brothers (right), stationers and printers at Burlington House, were the proprietors of the *Newquay Guardian* and the *Handbook to Newquay and North Cornwall.* Motor coach tours to other Cornish resorts are advertised opposite.

NEWQUAY
Tolcarne Beach 1925 78874

The sands of Tolcarne Beach, or Crigga, are crowded with holidaymakers, whose comforts are catered for by teashops and abundant beach tents. Strolling pedestrians observe the beach from the cliff top along Narrowcliff Road. The open space of the Barrowfields behind is still preserved for the benefit of all.

NEWQUAY
The Beach 1925
78867

This was for many years the popular image of surfing and bathing at Newquay, when plywood surfboards were the order of the day - this was long before the coming of wetsuits and fibreglass longboards and bodyboards. The beach is probably Tolcarne.

NEWQUAY, *Bathing Belles 1925* 78880

These bathers pose at the water's edge on one of Newquay's beaches, while other holidaymakers explore the rocks below the cliffs at low tide or just sit around relaxing. The fashions contrast with those seen in earlier times.

NEWQUAY
Bishop's Rock and the Headland 1901 47736

Overdressed holidaymakers in sun hats enjoy the sands in this view from Great Western Beach towards the Atlantic Hotel on the headland of the Beacon.

NEWQUAY
Towan Beach 1901
47734

Hotels and boarding houses stand right on the cliff edge overlooking the beach and harbour area. Towan Beach is the closest to the town centre; here, wheeled bathing machines have been drawn down to the edge of the sea, while a few beach tents and deckchairs are also provided for visitors. Long skirts and parasols are the fashion for the ladies.

NEWQUAY, *The Island and the Beacon 1912* 64791

This landmark at Towan Beach becomes a true island at high tide. A house was built here and connected to the mainland by a suspension footbridge in the early 20th century. The sails of fishing boats can be seen in the harbour on the far left below the Beacon and Atlantic Hotel.

NEWQUAY
The Atlantic Hotel 1922 72870

Glimpsed from the rocks below the Island, this great hotel was built in 1893 on the Beacon; it continues to dominate the Newquay scene over a century later, although it has lost some of its chimneys. The skyline is also broken on the right by the Huer's House, a pilchard fishermen's lookout, while to the left is the new war memorial, unveiled by the Duke of Cornwall in 1921.

NEWQUAY
The Harbour 1904
52297

Sailing schooners, typical coastal traders of their day, lie alongside the island pier in the harbour. The whiteness on the wall suggests that they are loading china clay, which was brought from St Austell by railway trucks run out across the wooden bridge. Sailors are taking the opportunity to maintain the three-master's underside at low tide.

NEWQUAY
The Harbour 1912
64787

Fishing boats, still all sailing craft at this date, are moored in the shelter of the two piers. Low tide has joined together all the sandy beaches in the background, with Tolcarne, Great Western and Towan seen from left to right.

NEWQUAY
Towan Head 1907 59325

The exposed headland separating Newquay Bay and Fistral Bay has always been a popular walk from the town. The lifeboat house in the distance (centre) was built in 1899 to replace an earlier station. It was closed in 1934, but it had a brief reprieve during the Second World War. Newquay had its first lifeboat in 1860.

NEWQUAY
Fistral Beach 1918
68639

Fistral is the wildest of Newquay's beaches, as it faces the open sea to the west. In contrast with the other beaches, here at the north end it is largely undeveloped except for the great block of the Headland Hotel, which was opened in 1900 to rival the equally large Atlantic Hotel. There is no promenade, and just a few beach tents are lined up on the beach below the sand dunes.

NEWQUAY
Pentire 1918 68647

This is at the south end of Fistral Beach, where visitors are walking out to picnic on East Pentire Point. The encroaching houses of Newquay have been stemmed by the golf links and dunes on the left, but piecemeal housing developments have already begun at Pentire or West Newquay. Today, though, the road is lined with hotels and houses.

NEWQUAY
The National Children's Home, Pentire 1918 68655

We are looking towards East Pentire Point, with a glimpse of the sea, the Gannel and Crantock Beach on the left. The sheep grazing in a field show that at this time Pentire was still a rural part of Newquay; but a very different scene meets the eye today. The National Children's Home, in the centre, has become the Tregarn Hotel, and is now surrounded by housing.

NEWQUAY
The Gannel 1925 78896

Houses have been built at Pentire on prime sites overlooking the Gannel. The attractive estuary is seen here at low tide, but deep pools in the sand make it a tricky place to cross over to Crantock. Small ferry boats are available to take the pedestrians when the tide is in.

NEWQUAY
The Gannel 1925
78897

The wooden footbridge over the main river channel allows pedestrians to gain the sands of the Gannel at low tide. This is summer, and haymaking is taking place in the field of Trethellan Farm behind.

NEWQUAY
The Gannel Regatta 1928 81296

Spectators on both sides of the Gannel are enjoying the annual August regatta. How different the Gannel looks at full tide. There were once plans to build a dam to keep water in the Gannel all the time as an amenity. This view looks from the Crantock side; most of the open fields on the Newquay side have since been covered with houses.

NEWQUAY, *Trenance Park and the Viaduct 1912* 64816

The attractive Trenance Gardens were developed in this sheltered valley which emerges near the head of the Gannel. Shady walks, seats, shelters, ponds for toy boats and a boating lake were all laid out for the pleasure of townsfolk and visitors. The Trenance Viaduct behind takes the railway into Newquay station. Its iron girders were replaced in 1939 with stone arches.

NEWQUAY
Tolcarne Cross 1907
59340

This granite cross was restored by Sir Robert Edgecumbe, according to the plaque on the base. It stands in front of a typical Cornish hedge, with slates built in a 'curzey-way' pattern capped with turf. This was on the edge of town in 1907 with nothing but fields behind; now there are a bowling club, tennis courts and houses.

ST COLUMB MINOR
The Village 1904
52536

The tall tower of the 14th-century St Columba's Church rises over the houses. This photograph was taken before the village was reached by the growth of Newquay's suburbs. It was then surrounded by countryside - note the unusual shape of the haystacks. St Columba's was the mother church of Newquay until St Michael's Church was built within the expanding town in 1857.

NEWQUAY, *Trerice Manor House 1912* 64817

This historic house, which dates from 1572, stands inland from Newquay. It was the home of the Arundell family, but it is now owned by the National Trust. This is a charming scene, with skittles set out in front of the main door, but the house has lost some of its former glory, for the right-hand wing is ruinous, and carved masonry is piled on the lawn. This photograph is of special interest because the derelict wing has since been fully restored.

CRANTOCK AND CUBERT

CRANTOCK
The Post Office c1955 C181009

The tiny post office could be easily missed were it not for the sign outside the cottage. The peace of the village is now broken during the summer by motorists seeking the sands of Crantock Beach, which is in a much quieter location than Newquay. Crantock is also close enough to Newquay for visitors to walk here by crossing the Gannel on foot or by ferry boat.

CRANTOCK
The Village 1918
68679

A very pretty scene with thatched cottages and not a soul in sight. How different from today!

CRANTOCK
The War Memorial 1922 72866

It is just four years after No 68679 (above) and the village war memorial has been built at the same spot. It takes the form of a small memorial hall, with a cross and five names of the fallen over the door. How sad that a further ten names were added after the next conflict.

CRANTOCK, *The Church 1904* 52311

The church of St Carantoc stands in its churchyard within sight of the sea. It has an unusual layout, with the chancel roof higher than the nave. Churchgate Cottage is the neat white building in the centre, but behind it near the lychgate we can see a roofless cottage, now at the end of the Old Albion Inn.

CRANTOCK
The Stocks 1912 64822

The shelter over the ancient wooden stocks in the churchyard appears to be newly erected in this photograph. William Tinney was the last man to be put in them, after robbing a Cubert widow in about 1817. He escaped, and used the tenor bell rope to make his escape from the church tower in which the stocks were secured. He went off to sea, and never returned.

CRANTOCK
The Village 1928 81288

The motoring age comes to Crantock. A variety of cars are parked haphazardly on the rough ground on the edge of the dunes by visitors who have braved the narrow descent from the village. There has been little development closer to the beach, and the village church's distinctive outline stands out on the skyline.

CRANTOCK
The West Pentire Hotel 1936 87613

The West Pentire Hotel is a conspicuous landmark in this otherwise bleak view across fields to the sea beyond Crantock Beach, with East Pentire Point on the right. The fields remain undeveloped today, although the hotel is now called the Crantock Bay Hotel.

CRANTOCK
The Gannel c1960 C181044

The presence of the Gannel has stopped Newquay from spilling over to Crantock. The massed houses at East Pentire on the Newquay side make a great contrast with the untouched dunes of the Rushy Green on the Crantock side.

CUBERT, *The Village c1960* C411014

The village stands on a high ridge to the south of Crantock, where the church is a landmark. It is noted for its tower with a low spire, unusual in Cornwall, which was struck by lightning in 1848 and later repaired. The church is now surrounded by housing.

CUBERT
The Post Office c1960
C411016

The village is situated astride the lane to Holywell Bay. Here the post office in the centre is displaying pottery and postcards to entice the passing visitors. It is nice to report that the post office store survives in an altered form, although the shop on the right is now a house. The bus stop by the water tap on the left has since been replaced by a shelter.

PERRANPORTH AND ST AGNES

PERRANPORTH
The Buried Church 1893 31835

By tradition, this small oratory of the 6th century is associated with St Piran. It was lost under the dunes of Penhale Sands until it was rediscovered and excavated in 1835. It is seen here surrounded by iron railings, and light sand has blown like snow onto the walls. The precious ruin was later protected within a concrete shell, but it has subsequently been reburied for protection. A medieval church nearby was also lost in the sands.

PERRANPORTH
Perran Sands Holiday Camp c1960 P43074

This is camping and caravanning 1960s-style, when basic facilities included a small camp shop and the licensed Perran Sands Club. This spot is unrecognisable today among the trappings of a modern holiday park.

PERRANPORTH, *From the Sandhills 1893* 31821

Perranporth was undeveloped in the 1890s, with just a scattering of houses, but it was becoming popular for bathing on account of its vast beach. The large building in its own grounds commanding the beach is the Ponsmere Hotel. Perranporth was a once a mining village, but the chimneys on the skyline, extreme left, belong to Nobel's Explosives Works, which was located up on the cliffs away from habitation.

PERRANPORTH, *The Lake 1925* 78909

The railway line, which we can see in the foreground, boosted the development of Perranporth as a resort. It was opened in 1903, but it was closed exactly 60 years later. St Michael's Church of 1872 is behind the embankment to the right. There is some activity on the boating lake, but most visitors have come for the delights of the long expanse of golden sands. The dunes rise above, while in the distance are silhouetted the old engine houses of the Penhale Mine.

PERRANPORTH
The Rocks 1912 64836

Like so many visitors before and after them, two little girls are exploring the fascinating caves and arches in the cliffs under Droskyn Point, which become accessible to walkers on the sands at low tide. They are partly natural, but mostly result from old mine workings into the cliffs.

PERRANPORTH
Tywarnhayle Square c1960
P43037

There is some motoring activity, with the cars parked before the days of double yellow lines and other restrictions. The 'keep left' sign and roundabout (centre) is a period piece. A O Tabb's Central Stores and the Flower Shop (behind the roundabout) have since become a Spa store, but the Strand House newsagent's (left) is still there.

PERRANPORTH
The Hotel 1890
23967

Here we see a part of Perranporth in its early days as a tourist resort, with few houses, no traffic and just two people posed on the footbridge. The hotel stands between the Perrancoombe stream and St George's Hill, which takes the road up towards St Agnes.

PERRANPORTH
Boscawen Park 1938 88798

The palm trees add an exotic touch to the park in this view, which looks in a similar direction to the 1890 view (No 23967 on page 43). By this date the open spaces have been infilled with housing, and the Perranporth Hotel can be recognised on the far side of the pond immediately behind the right-hand tree.

MITHIAN
Harmony Cottage c1950 M227012

The esteemed painter John Opie was born at Harmony Cot in May 1761. Although the son of a carpenter, his painting skills were recognised by Dr Wolcot, who took him to London; there he became a famous portrait painter and a professor at the Royal Academy. He died in 1807, and was buried in St Paul's Cathedral.

MITHIAN
The Village c1950 M227005

Mithian lies just off the Perranporth to St Agnes road. Here at the top end of the hamlet, the nearest end of the thatched house is the post office, with a telephone kiosk outside. The very small village hall is on the left.

ST AGNES
The St Agnes Hotel c1955
S390063

The hotel is the largest building in the centre of town, and was built to serve the holiday trade. Next door an awning shades Martins Stores from the sun, while across the street is a baker's and confectioner's shop (centre), which has since become a gift shop. The lych gate for St Agnes parish church is opposite the hotel (right).

ST AGNES
Town Hill c1955
S390020

Fortunately, there is no traffic as the farmer herds his small herd of cows in the middle of the road at the bottom of Town Hill beside the Peterville Inn. The beacon symbol on the school sign on the left is a nostalgic reminder of the past.

ST AGNES, *Peterville Hill c1955* S390039

Nothing changes. The same cows are being herded in almost the same place as No. 390020 (page 46) in this view looking the opposite way. The Peterville Inn, which has since acquired a wide porch, stands by the junction with Quay Road leading to Trevaunance Cove to the right of the camera. All is quiet in this scene, but increasing traffic congestion, both local and tourist, finally led to the narrow hill becoming a one-way street.

ST AGNES
Rocky Lane and St Agnes Cove c1955
S390013

This view is almost timeless. The gravel track winds steeply down between slopes covered in bracken and gorse, with an enticing glimpse of the beach and rugged cliffs beyond. We are reminded that this is also a mining landscape by the large waste tip of Wheal Kitty tin mine on the extreme right.

ST AGNES

The Beach c1955 S390050

The beach is seen at low tide, with dramatic crumbling cliffs towering up behind. A few small boats can be launched from trolleys at the slipway beside the beach shop and Cove Café, which satisfy the needs of the holidaymakers.

ST AGNES
The Cliff Shelter c1955 S390032

There is little room on the beach at St Agnes or Trevaunance Cove at high tide, and neither is there much space for houses on the cliff above. The public shelter is perched on the only available ground overlooking the beach. The tiny harbour serving the mines was destroyed in a storm, but the granite blocks of its pier can be seen lying as rubble at the sea's edge.

ST AGNES, *The Cliffs at Chapel Porth c1955* S390015

The old Wheal Coates mine, perched on the steep cliffs of St Agnes Head, has been frequently photographed over the years. Such a dramatic combination of sea, cliffs and ruined engine houses is instantly recognised as part of the Cornish landscape. Low tide reveals a large expanse of golden sand here at Chapel Porth.

PORTHTOWAN AND PORTREATH

PORTHTOWAN
Western Cliff 1925 78615

Here we see Porthtowan in its early days as a resort, with just a few homes on the hillside, a line of chalets, two bell tents and an open charabanc among the parked vehicles. This is still essentially a valley devastated by years of mining activity, evidenced by the disturbed ground in the foreground and the old engine house between the cliff and the beach.

PORTHTOWAN
Eastern Cliff 1935
86591

It is ten years after No 78615 on page 50, and we are looking the other way, with the rough valley floor not yet developed with shops, flats and a car park. A bell tent and two caravans are in the foreground, and holiday chalets are marching over the far hillside. The good surf on the beach shows why Porthtowan has now become popular for surfing.

PORTHTOWAN, *The Village c1960* P88073

This might be considered to be the heart of the village, with the large building containing a bed and breakfast establishment and a provisions shop next door. The Commodore Inn (now the Unicorn) stands in the centre of the view, with the village hall on the right.

PORTREATH, *The Harbour 1890* 23030

Portreath was a busy mining port in the 19th century, when sailing vessels loaded copper ore for the Welsh smelters and returned with coal for the mine engines. A rough sea is coming onto the beach, but the pier affords protection to the dangerously narrow harbour entrance beneath the cliffs. Shipping had much declined by this date, and the quays are becoming derelict. The white daymark on the headland guided ships towards the harbour.

PORTREATH
The Docks 1898 41628

Three steam coasters have discharged their cargo of coal, which is heaped on the quayside. The nearest ship is the *Coniston Fell*, one of the colliers belonging to D W Bain, who controlled the harbour at that time. A crane in the foreground lowers timber balks across the basin entrance to give protection from rough seas. The white building on the left is the harbourmaster's house, and the inclined plane of the railway from Camborne and its mines descends between the terraced houses in the background.

PORTREATH
The Beach Car Park c1955 P95001

Here is a fine line-up of period cars overlooking the beach at Portreath. It is a place to sit on a bench in the sunshine or to stay in the car and admire the view of the beach and sea. The dock basins, with the harbourmaster's house, are beyond the wall.

PORTREATH
Hell's Mouth c1960 P95011

The ubiquitous herring gull poses for the camera above Hell's Mouth, an awesome cleft that has become a place to visit because of its close proximity to the coast road between Portreath and Gwithian.

HAYLE AND ST IVES BAY

GODREVY ISLAND
The Lighthouse 1890 24194

The lighthouse guards the northern end of St Ives Bay. Its octagonal tower was built by James Walker in 1859 after a series of shipwrecks on the offshore reef known as the Stones. Trinity House keepers lived on the island until 1934, when the light became automatic. A long camera exposure gives the appearance of a flat sea, but during big storms the spray can break over the top of the lantern.

GWITHIAN
The Village c1960
G187037

The church of St Gocianus has a 15th-century granite tower, but much of the rest was rebuilt in 1866. This location has a long history. An early Christian oratory was discovered in the sands in the 19th century, but it has been reburied. The Old Parsonage is the building on the right.

HAYLE, *Towans and the Beach 1927* 80084

Just sitting and looking about or wandering around splashing in the natural pool are the main activities for these holidaymakers. The tide is well out, revealing the great expanse of Hayle Sands. On the horizon is the distinctive outline of Godrevy Island off Godrevy Point.

HAYLE
Towans and the Paddling Pool 1925
78626

A traditional seaside pastime for children is paddling about in pools left behind by the falling tide. All the children have been told to stand still for this delightful photograph, while their parents look on behind. Holiday bungalows and chalets line the skyline, and the Cove Café is perched on a shelf halfway down the cliff (centre).

HAYLE

Towans, The Cove Café 1931 84150

All the seaside visitor needs is offered at the Cove Café, including teas, hot water, newspapers, telephone and deck chair hire. The café is well sited beside the path down to the beach, where a sign warns bathers of the dangers of the sea and a lifebuoy, lifejackets and lifeline are provided for emergencies.

HAYLE
Towans 1927 80090

Here we have a superb depiction of period bell tents and caravans for holidaymakers, pitched on the dunes overlooking the sea. The chalets and homes on the cliff edge have the best view across the water to Carbis Bay and St Ives Island. Knill's Steeple stands on the highest hill (on the horizon, left). Compared with modern campsites, this is car-free except for the little Austin 7 car on the right.

PHILLACK
The Village c1960
P354001

The village is on the north side of the Hayle estuary, and the water of Copperhouse Pool has kept its identity apart from the town of Hayle. Like Gwithian, this could be an early Christian site, for a carved chi-rho symbol (the first two Greek letters of the word 'Christ') of the 6th or 7th century is built into the gable of the south porch of the church.

PHILLACK
The New Inn c1960 P354005

The New Inn is a welcome haven in the centre of the small village, with its own car park at the side allowing calling motorists to leave the narrow street. The inn has been renamed The Bucket of Blood, which refers to the story that in the days when sailors and smugglers drank here, blood was found in the well, which led to the finding of a murdered revenue officer at the bottom.

HAYLE
Fore Street at Copperhouse 1892 29881

A small crowd of children poses outside Edwin Broad's draper's shop. This is a hot sunny day, as we can see from the shadows and the shop awnings. It could also be half-day closing, for the street is otherwise deserted. This part of Hayle is known as Copperhouse because there was a copper smelting works and foundry of that name here in the 18th and 19th centuries.

HAYLE
Fore Street 1927
80076

There is more activity in the street now, although the traffic is slight compared with modern times. Two cars are travelling up the street together, while a third is parked with a white-coated chauffeur in attendance. The Cornubia Hotel, in the background with its fine porch, remains part of the scene today.

HAYLE
Penpol Terrace 1892
29878

Two-masted schooners are laid up on the ground at low tide opposite the main South Quay. An old stone bollard in front of the sailing yacht (left) tells of busier days in the port. This is the Foundry part of Hayle, once dominated by Harvey & Co's famous foundry. Today, small shop developments have taken over the gardens at the front of the long Penpol Terrace.

HAYLE, *From Lelant 1928* 81198

Old fishing boats, some decommissioned, are beached on the foreshore on the Lelant side of the estuary. Rising above the rooftops over at Hayle is the church of St Elwyn (left), designed by J D Sedding and completed in 1888. Penpol Terrace is to its right, and in the middle distance is the Carnsew Pool, which was built with a sluice for flushing out the main channel.

LELANT
The Golf Links 1928
81194

The golf links are home to the West Cornwall Golf Club, the oldest in Cornwall. The lady golfer attempts a long put on the 4th green, while her partner holds a tall flagpole. The plus-fours and lightweight club bags are a far cry from the equipment of the modern golfer. Behind is Lelant's granite church of St Uny, which was once the mother church for St Ives. Tradition has it that there is a town buried beneath the sands of Lelant Towans.

LELANT
The Railway Station 1928 81197

The 4-mile branch line opened in 1877 from the main line at St Erth station to St Ives is one of the most scenic in the south-west. This tranquil scene shows the railway running alongside Lelant saltings on the Hayle estuary, where the rising tide will soon re-float the boats beached alongside an old quay. Although trains still stop here, the station building is now a private house.

LELANT, *Church Lane 1892* 29876

Granite cottages and walled gardens line the old lane leading invitingly to the church tower beyond. A small lad with a jug has managed to get into the picture and poses on a granite step.

CARBIS BAY
The Valley 1895
35846

These were the days when there was a rural community here, with a few cottages set among the fields around the narrow valley leading down to the beach at Carbis Bay. Houses belonging to the main village can be seen at the head of the valley.

CARBIS BAY, *General View 1901* 47688

This view shows Carbis Bay when it was still largely undeveloped, with just a scattering of houses above the cliffs overlooking the sandy beach. The scenic St Ives branch railway follows the coast, with a four-arched viaduct crossing the little valley behind the beach; the station platform is just beyond. The back of the Carbis Bay Hotel can be seen on the left.

CARBIS BAY, *The Beach and the Hotel 1922* 72860

The Carbis Bay Hotel was described as an 'excellent family hotel' at the turn of the century. It is extremely well sited just above the sandy beach; this beach is on the sheltered side of St Ives Bay, so the sea is calmer and better suited for bathing than the more exposed beaches. There is minimal development on the beach - just a hut advertising refreshments and Cadbury's chocolate.

CARBIS BAY
The Beach c1955
C22049

The refreshment hut has now been overtaken by a more substantial establishment, which offers outside seating and car parking on the beach. The sands are no longer deserted, but packed with holidaymakers, and new houses have appeared above the railway line in the background since the 1922 photograph (No 72860, page 68).

CARBIS BAY, *General View c1955* C22032

This view is given added interest because it is taken from the top of one of the large waste tips of the old Providence copper and tin mine, which closed in 1877. Collapsed shafts continue to cause problems in the residential areas built over the old workings. In the distance towards the right are the twin chimneys of the Hayle power station, since demolished, while to the left are the long sands of Hayle Towans.

ST IVES

ST IVES, *General View 1890* 23014

St Ives is seen from Draycott Terrace, overlooking cottages in Primrose Valley below and the curving sweep of the railway station beyond, most of which is now a car park. Seine fishing boats are drawn up on Porthminster Beach (right), and an old engine house stands on Pedn Olva Point. Large houses follow the Terrace and Trelyon Avenue, and on the extreme left the vacant grassy plot is the site of the Porthminster Hotel.

ST IVES
The Railway Station 1928 81179

A four-coach train stands in the station, which was the point of arrival for many visitors to St Ives - and what a location it had, just above the beach. Long since removed for a car park, the old station building has the usual enamel signs advertising Virol, Bovril and Wrights coal tar soap. A goods train is in the yard behind. Porthminster Hotel rises above the station, while to the left Draycott Terrace stands above the apartments which have replaced the Primrose Valley cottages.

ST IVES
Porthminster 1898
41609

The commanding position of the newly built Porthminster Hotel is seen in this view from the hill behind Draycott Terrace. Down by the railway viaduct we can see the numerous pilchard seine boats drawn up on Porthminster Beach, for this was a working beach before it became a pleasure beach.

ST IVES, *Draycott Terrace 1901* 47678

It is just three years after No 41609, above, and the Porthminster Hotel has been given an extension in the form of a smaller version of the original building. This is a steep site, and the road along the front of Draycott Terrace is supported by a substantial stone wall. The terraced cottages in Primrose Valley below are still intact.

ST IVES, *Porthminster Beach 1925* 78644

Lines of beach tents have taken over much of the beach, and by this date there are just a few remaining fishing boats drawn up above the high tide line.

ST IVES
Pedn Olva 1930
83337

This scene is at the end of Porthminster Beach, where steps lead down from the Warren and past the shelters built on the rocks. The house, in a prime site between the beach and the harbour, has been much extended as the Pednolva Hotel.

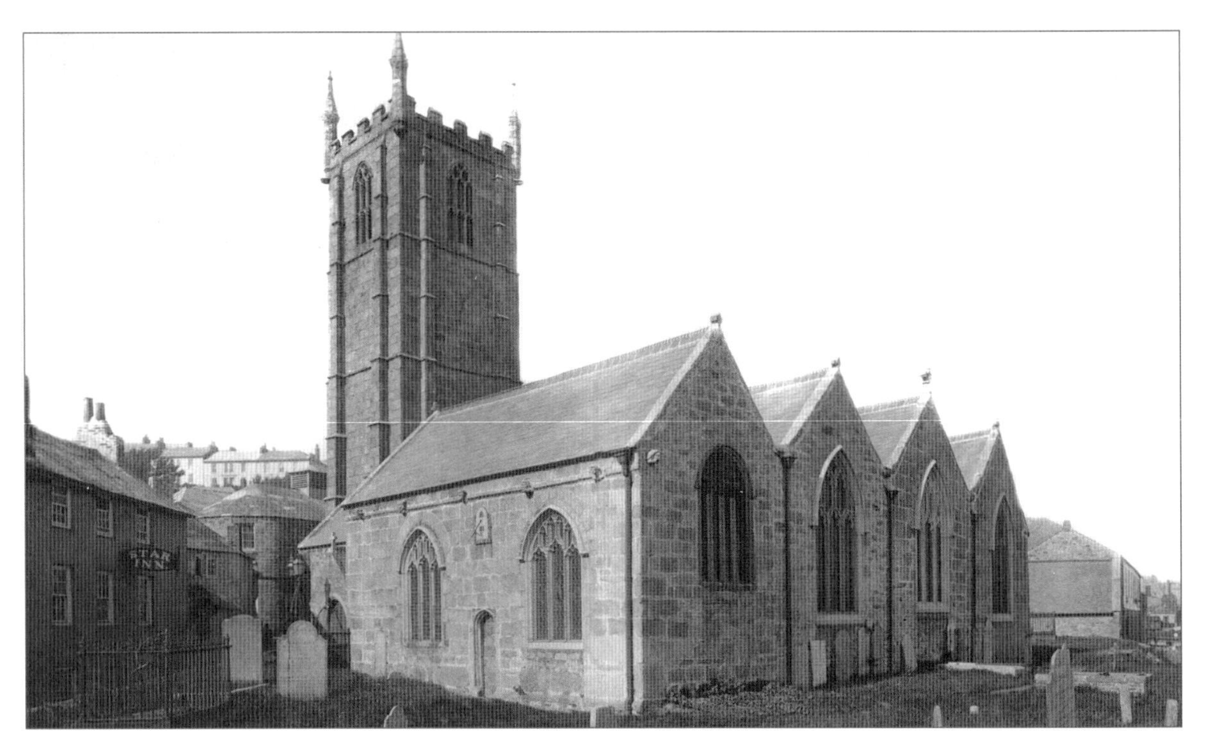

ST IVES, *The Church 1890* 23017

The early 15th-century church of St Ia is a prominent landmark in the harbour area. The church appears shortened in this unusual view because of the position of the south chapel in the foreground. On the left, the Star Inn and the building next door in St Andrew's Street have since made way for the town's war memorial and gardens, but the Market House glimpsed behind still survives.

ST IVES, *The Harbour 1895* 35830

The church could hardly be closer to the sea. Many of the buildings can be recognised today, but they are now separated from the water in the harbour by walls supporting a road and a walkway. The St Ives lifeboat is on its carriage outside the lifeboat house on West Pier near the church. The present lifeboat house is on the near side of the pier.

ST IVES, *The Harbour 1890* 24175

Rows of fishing boats are mostly aground where they are moored in the harbour. Smaller boats are drawn right up to the buildings in the background, for the Wharf wall had not yet been built. The whitewashed Fore Street Methodist chapel is to the right, likewise built onto the harbour beach.

ST IVES
The Harbour 1892
31158

Mackerel and pilchard luggers are afloat and drying their dark brown sails in the harbour. Their shape gives a good idea of the type of rig. By chance, the two lighthouses on Smeaton's Pier can be seen through the gaps behind. The pierhead one on the right was first lit two years earlier.

ST IVES, *The Harbour 1922* 72832

Some 30 years after No 31158, above, many of the fishing boats are now powered by motors. The days of sail were really over, and the boats were either converted or replaced with new craft. In the background the Wharf wall has been built all along the harbour from the West Pier.

C. JENKYN

ST IVES
The Fish Market 1925
78661

Fish catches are auctioned at the top of the slipway on the Wharf, watched by a small crowd of fishermen, merchants and interested passers-by. The Sloop Inn is in the background (centre right), with James Laity's grocery shop to its right and G Jenkyn's boot and shoe shop on the left. Except for the pub, all the other buildings now contain shops or restaurants for servicing the tourists.

ST IVES, *Gulls 1925* 78662

The seagulls are famous in St Ives; here they are gathering on the harbour beach waiting for scraps, while fishermen sort their catch using trestle tops and wicker fish baskets. On the far left one of the port's fishermen's lodges stands on the Wharf. The elaborate building above the rowing boat is James Laity's grocery store, once a delight to visit.

ST IVES, *Wharf Road c1955* S22040

The Wharf road was established behind a harbour wall in 1922 to protect this part of town from the sea, while also improving vehicular access. It incorporates part of an earlier slipway in the foreground, while further on the projecting structure is a bandstand. At the far end, the Mariners' Church looms above the Methodist chapel, which stands incongruously in a line of restaurants and cafés along the Wharf. The nearest building is Lanham's Harbour Sale Room, since converted to the Lifeboat Inn.

ST IVES
The Harbour c1955 S22038

Artists are now attracted to the harbour scene, but there are far fewer fishing boats than in earlier days. Prominent buildings include the parish church behind West Pier and the rectangular block of Woolworth's in the centre of the Wharf.

ST IVES
The Island from Man's Head 1890
24180

The Island, topped with St Nicholas' Chapel, and the undeveloped beach at Porthmeor, are seen from the coast path at Man's Head or Carrick Du. This last view of the sea has the added interest of the ruined engine house of Carrick Du copper mine, built in 1854 for a 36-inch cylinder pumping engine, standing by the tiny enclosures with rough stone walls on the very cliff edge.

ST IVES, *St John's Church 1890* 24190

St John's in the Fields was built in 1846 to the design of the architect J P St Aubyn at Hellesvean, which lies up the hill to the west of St Ives. It still has its rural setting in this photograph, which was taken over 40 years later.

ST IVES
The Tregenna Castle Hotel 1890 23024

Tregenna Castle was built as a house for John Stephens in 1774 to the designs of John Wood the younger, the well-known architect of Georgian Bath. It stands above the town, and has staggering views over the Bay, so it is little wonder that the Great Western Railway turned it into a hotel.

ST IVES, *The John Knill Monument 1908* 61085

John Knill (1733-1811) intended this monument on a high hill outside St Ives to be his mausoleum, but he was buried in London. He left a legacy for a celebration to be held in his memory every five years on St James's Day (25 July), when 10 girls in white with two widows, a fiddler, the parson, a customs officer and the mayor parade here. The visible face of the three-sided granite steeple is inscribed: 'Resurgam' ('I shall rise again') above his coat-of-arms, while 'Johannes Knill 1782' and 'I know that my redeemer liveth' are inscribed on the other faces.

INDEX

Frith Book Co Titles

www.francisfrith.co.uk

The Frith Book Company publishes over 100 new titles each year. A selection of those currently available is listed below. For latest catalogue please contact Frith Book Co.
Town Books 96 pages, approximately 100 photos. ***County and Themed Books*** 128 pages, approximately 150 photos (unless specified). All titles hardback with laminated case and jacket, except those indicated pb (paperback)

Title	ISBN	Price
Amersham, Chesham & Rickmansworth (pb)	1-85937-340-2	£9.99
Andover (pb)	1-85937-292-9	£9.99
Aylesbury (pb)	1-85937-227-9	£9.99
Barnstaple (pb)	1-85937-300-3	£9.99
Basildon Living Memories (pb)	1-85937-515-4	£9.99
Bath (pb)	1-85937-419-0	£9.99
Bedford (pb)	1-85937-205-8	£9.99
Bedfordshire Living Memories	1-85937-513-8	£14.99
Belfast (pb)	1-85937-303-8	£9.99
Berkshire (pb)	1-85937-191-4	£9.99
Berkshire Churches	1-85937-170-1	£17.99
Berkshire Living Memories	1-85937-332-1	£14.99
Black Country	1-85937-497-2	£12.99
Blackpool (pb)	1-85937-393-3	£9.99
Bognor Regis (pb)	1-85937-431-x	£9.99
Bournemouth (pb)	1-85937-545-6	£9.99
Bradford (pb)	1-85937-204-x	£9.99
Bridgend (pb)	1-85937-386-0	£7.99
Bridgwater (pb)	1-85937-305-4	£9.99
Bridport (pb)	1-85937-327-5	£9.99
Brighton (pb)	1-85937-192-2	£8.99
Bristol (pb)	1-85937-264-3	£9.99
British Life A Century Ago (pb)	1-85937-213-9	£9.99
Buckinghamshire (pb)	1-85937-200-7	£9.99
Camberley (pb)	1-85937-222-8	£9.99
Cambridge (pb)	1-85937-422-0	£9.99
Cambridgeshire (pb)	1-85937-420-4	£9.99
Cambridgeshire Villages	1-85937-523-5	£14.99
Canals And Waterways (pb)	1-85937-291-0	£9.99
Canterbury Cathedral (pb)	1-85937-179-5	£9.99
Cardiff (pb)	1-85937-093-4	£9.99
Carmarthenshire (pb)	1-85937-604-5	£9.99
Chelmsford (pb)	1-85937-310-0	£9.99
Cheltenham (pb)	1-85937-095-0	£9.99
Cheshire (pb)	1-85937-271-6	£9.99
Chester (pb)	1-85937-382 8	£9.99
Chesterfield (pb)	1-85937-378-x	£9.99
Chichester (pb)	1-85937-228-7	£9.99
Churches of East Cornwall (pb)	1-85937-249-x	£9.99
Churches of Hampshire (pb)	1-85937-207-4	£9.99
Cinque Ports & Two Ancient Towns	1-85937-492-1	£14.99
Colchester (pb)	1-85937-188-4	£8.99
Cornwall (pb)	1-85937-229-5	£9.99
Cornwall Living Memories	1-85937-248-1	£14.99
Cotswolds (pb)	1-85937-230-9	£9.99
Cotswolds Living Memories	1-85937-255-4	£14.99
County Durham (pb)	1-85937-398-4	£9.99
Croydon Living Memories (pb)	1-85937-162-0	£9.99
Cumbria (pb)	1-85937-621-5	£9.99
Derby (pb)	1-85937-367-4	£9.99
Derbyshire (pb)	1-85937-196-5	£9.99
Derbyshire Living Memories	1-85937-330-5	£14.99
Devon (pb)	1-85937-297-x	£9.99
Devon Churches (pb)	1-85937-250-3	£9.99
Dorchester (pb)	1-85937-307-0	£9.99
Dorset (pb)	1-85937-269-4	£9.99
Dorset Coast (pb)	1-85937-299-6	£9.99
Dorset Living Memories (pb)	1-85937-584-7	£9.99
Down the Severn (pb)	1-85937-560-x	£9.99
Down The Thames (pb)	1-85937-278-3	£9.99
Down the Trent	1-85937-311-9	£14.99
East Anglia (pb)	1-85937-265-1	£9.99
East Grinstead (pb)	1-85937-138-8	£9.99
East London	1-85937-080-2	£14.99
East Sussex (pb)	1-85937-606-1	£9.99
Eastbourne (pb)	1-85937-399-2	£9.99
Edinburgh (pb)	1-85937-193-0	£8.99
England In The 1880s	1-85937-331-3	£17.99
Essex - Second Selection	1-85937-456-5	£14.99
Essex (pb)	1-85937-270-8	£9.99
Essex Coast	1-85937-342-9	£14.99
Essex Living Memories	1-85937-490-5	£14.99
Exeter	1-85937-539-1	£9.99
Exmoor (pb)	1-85937-608-8	£9.99
Falmouth (pb)	1-85937-594-4	£9.99
Folkestone (pb)	1-85937-124-8	£9.99
Frome (pb)	1-85937-317-8	£9.99
Glamorgan	1-85937-488-3	£14.99
Glasgow (pb)	1-85937-190-6	£9.99
Glastonbury (pb)	1-85937-338-0	£7.99
Gloucester (pb)	1-85937-232-5	£9.99
Gloucestershire (pb)	1-85937-561-8	£9.99
Great Yarmouth (pb)	1-85937-426-3	£9.99
Greater Manchester (pb)	1-85937-266-x	£9.99
Guildford (pb)	1-85937-410-7	£9.99
Hampshire (pb)	1-85937-279-1	£9.99
Harrogate (pb)	1-85937-423-9	£9.99
Hastings and Bexhill (pb)	1-85937-131-0	£9.99
Heart of Lancashire (pb)	1-85937-197-3	£9.99
Helston (pb)	1-85937-214-7	£9.99
Hereford (pb)	1-85937-175-2	£9.99
Herefordshire (pb)	1-85937-567-7	£9.99
Herefordshire Living Memories	1-85937-514-6	£14.99
Hertfordshire (pb)	1-85937-247-3	£9.99
Horsham (pb)	1-85937-432-8	£9.99
Humberside (pb)	1-85937-605-3	£9.99
Hythe, Romney Marsh, Ashford (pb)	1-85937-256-2	£9.99
Ipswich (pb)	1-85937-424-7	£9.99
Isle of Man (pb)	1-85937-268-6	£9.99
Isle of Wight (pb)	1-85937-429-8	£9.99
Isle of Wight Living Memories	1-85937-304-6	£14.99
Kent (pb)	1-85937-189-2	£9.99
Kent Living Memories(pb)	1-85937-401-8	£9.99
Kings Lynn (pb)	1-85937-334-8	£9.99

Available from your local bookshop or from the publisher

Frith Book Co Titles (continued)

Title	ISBN	Price
Lake District (pb)	1-85937-275-9	£9.99
Lancashire Living Memories	1-85937-335-6	£14.99
Lancaster, Morecambe, Heysham (pb)	1-85937-233-3	£9.99
Leeds (pb)	1-85937-202-3	£9.99
Leicester (pb)	1-85937-381-x	£9.99
Leicestershire & Rutland Living Memories	1-85937-500-6	£12.99
Leicestershire (pb)	1-85937-185-x	£9.99
Lighthouses	1-85937-257-0	£9.99
Lincoln (pb)	1-85937-380-1	£9.99
Lincolnshire (pb)	1-85937-433-6	£9.99
Liverpool and Merseyside (pb)	1-85937-234-1	£9.99
London (pb)	1-85937-183-3	£9.99
London Living Memories	1-85937-454-9	£14.99
Ludlow (pb)	1-85937-176-0	£9.99
Luton (pb)	1-85937-235-x	£9.99
Maidenhead (pb)	1-85937-339-9	£9.99
Maidstone (pb)	1-85937-391-7	£9.99
Manchester (pb)	1-85937-198-1	£9.99
Marlborough (pb)	1-85937-336-4	£9.99
Middlesex	1-85937-158-2	£14.99
Monmouthshire	1-85937-532-4	£14.99
New Forest (pb)	1-85937-390-9	£9.99
Newark (pb)	1-85937-366-6	£9.99
Newport, Wales (pb)	1-85937-258-9	£9.99
Newquay (pb)	1-85937-421-2	£9.99
Norfolk (pb)	1-85937-195-7	£9.99
Norfolk Broads	1-85937-486-7	£14.99
Norfolk Living Memories (pb)	1-85937-402-6	£9.99
North Buckinghamshire	1-85937-626-6	£14.99
North Devon Living Memories	1-85937-261-9	£14.99
North Hertfordshire	1-85937-547-2	£14.99
North London (pb)	1-85937-403-4	£9.99
North Somerset	1-85937-302-x	£14.99
North Wales (pb)	1-85937-298-8	£9.99
North Yorkshire (pb)	1-85937-236-8	£9.99
Northamptonshire Living Memories	1-85937-529-4	£14.99
Northamptonshire	1-85937-150-7	£14.99
Northumberland Tyne & Wear (pb)	1-85937-281-3	£9.99
Northumberland	1-85937-522-7	£14.99
Norwich (pb)	1-85937-194-9	£8.99
Nottingham (pb)	1-85937-324-0	£9.99
Nottinghamshire (pb)	1-85937-187-6	£9.99
Oxford (pb)	1-85937-411-5	£9.99
Oxfordshire (pb)	1-85937-430-1	£9.99
Oxfordshire Living Memories	1-85937-525-1	£14.99
Paignton (pb)	1-85937-374-7	£7.99
Peak District (pb)	1-85937-280-5	£9.99
Pembrokeshire	1-85937-262-7	£14.99
Penzance (pb)	1-85937-595-2	£9.99
Peterborough (pb)	1-85937-219-8	£9.99
Picturesque Harbours	1-85937-208-2	£14.99
Piers	1-85937-237-6	£17.99
Plymouth (pb)	1-85937-389-5	£9.99
Poole & Sandbanks (pb)	1-85937-251-1	£9.99
Preston (pb)	1-85937-212-0	£9.99
Reading (pb)	1-85937-238-4	£9.99
Redhill to Reigate (pb)	1-85937-596-0	£9.99
Ringwood (pb)	1-85937-384-4	£7.99
Romford (pb)	1-85937-319-4	£9.99
Royal Tunbridge Wells (pb)	1-85937-504-9	£9.99
Salisbury (pb)	1-85937-239-2	£9.99
Scarborough (pb)	1-85937-379-8	£9.99
Sevenoaks and Tonbridge (pb)	1-85937-392-5	£9.99
Sheffield & South Yorks (pb)	1-85937-267-8	£9.99
Sherborne (pb)	1-85937-301-1	£9.99
Shrewsbury (pb)	1-85937-325-9	£9.99
Shropshire (pb)	1-85937-326-7	£9.99
Shropshire Living Memories	1-85937-643-6	£14.99
Somerset	1-85937-153-1	£14.99
South Devon Coast	1-85937-107-8	£14.99
South Devon Living Memories (pb)	1-85937-609-6	£9.99
South East London (pb)	1-85937-263-5	£9.99
South Somerset	1-85937-318-6	£14.99
South Wales	1-85937-519-7	£14.99
Southampton (pb)	1-85937-427-1	£9.99
Southend (pb)	1-85937-313-5	£9.99
Southport (pb)	1-85937-425-5	£9.99
St Albans (pb)	1-85937-341-0	£9.99
St Ives (pb)	1-85937-415-8	£9.99
Stafford Living Memories (pb)	1-85937-503-0	£9.99
Staffordshire (pb)	1-85937-308-9	£9.99
Stourbridge (pb)	1-85937-530-8	£9.99
Stratford upon Avon (pb)	1-85937-388-7	£9.99
Suffolk (pb)	1-85937-221-x	£9.99
Suffolk Coast (pb)	1-85937-610-x	£9.99
Surrey (pb)	1-85937-240-6	£9.99
Surrey Living Memories	1-85937-328-3	£14.99
Sussex (pb)	1-85937-184-1	£9.99
Sutton (pb)	1-85937-337-2	£9.99
Swansea (pb)	1-85937-167-1	£9.99
Taunton (pb)	1-85937-314-3	£9.99
Tees Valley & Cleveland (pb)	1-85937-623-1	£9.99
Teignmouth (pb)	1-85937-370-4	£7.99
Thanet (pb)	1-85937-116-7	£9.99
Tiverton (pb)	1-85937-178-7	£9.99
Torbay (pb)	1-85937-597-9	£9.99
Truro (pb)	1-85937-598-7	£9.99
Victorian & Edwardian Dorset	1-85937-254-6	£14.99
Victorian & Edwardian Kent (pb)	1-85937-624-X	£9.99
Victorian & Edwardian Maritime Album (pb)	1-85937-622-3	£9.99
Victorian and Edwardian Sussex (pb)	1-85937-625-8	£9.99
Villages of Devon (pb)	1-85937-293-7	£9.99
Villages of Kent (pb)	1-85937-294-5	£9.99
Villages of Sussex (pb)	1-85937-295-3	£9.99
Warrington (pb)	1-85937-507-3	£9.99
Warwick (pb)	1-85937-518-9	£9.99
Warwickshire (pb)	1-85937-203-1	£9.99
Welsh Castles (pb)	1-85937-322-4	£9.99
West Midlands (pb)	1-85937-289-9	£9.99
West Sussex (pb)	1-85937-607-x	£9.99
West Yorkshire (pb)	1-85937-201-5	£9.99
Weston Super Mare (pb)	1-85937-306-2	£9.99
Weymouth (pb)	1-85937-209-0	£9.99
Wiltshire (pb)	1-85937-277-5	£9.99
Wiltshire Churches (pb)	1-85937-171-x	£9.99
Wiltshire Living Memories (pb)	1-85937-396-8	£9.99
Winchester (pb)	1-85937-428-x	£9.99
Windsor (pb)	1-85937-333-x	£9.99
Wokingham & Bracknell (pb)	1-85937-329-1	£9.99
Woodbridge (pb)	1-85937-498-0	£9.99
Worcester (pb)	1-85937-165-5	£9.99
Worcestershire Living Memories	1-85937-489-1	£14.99
Worcestershire	1-85937-152-3	£14.99
York (pb)	1-85937-199-x	£9.99
Yorkshire (pb)	1-85937-186-8	£9.99
Yorkshire Coastal Memories	1-85937-506-5	£14.99
Yorkshire Dales	1-85937-502-2	£14.99
Yorkshire Living Memories (pb)	1-85937-397-6	£9.99

See Frith books on the internet at www.francisfrith.co.uk

FRITH PRODUCTS & SERVICES

Francis Frith would doubtless be pleased to know that the pioneering publishing venture he started in 1860 still continues today. Over a hundred and forty years later, The Francis Frith Collection continues in the same innovative tradition and is now one of the foremost publishers of vintage photographs in the world. Some of the current activities include:

Interior Decoration

Today Frith's photographs can be seen framed and as giant wall murals in thousands of pubs, restaurants, hotels, banks, retail stores and other public buildings throughout the country. In every case they enhance the unique local atmosphere of the places they depict and provide reminders of gentler days in an increasingly busy and frenetic world.

Product Promotions

Frith products are used by many major companies to promote the sales of their own products or to reinforce their own history and heritage. Frith promotions have been used by Hovis bread, Courage beers, Scots Porage Oats, Colman's mustard, Cadbury's foods, Mellow Birds coffee, Dunhill pipe tobacco, Guinness, and Bulmer's Cider.

Genealogy and Family History

As the interest in family history and roots grows world-wide, more and more people are turning to Frith's photographs of Great Britain for images of the towns, villages and streets where their ancestors lived; and, of course, photographs of the churches and chapels where their ancestors were christened, married and buried are an essential part of every genealogy tree and family album.

Frith Products

All Frith photographs are available Framed or just as Mounted Prints and Posters (size 23 x 16 inches). These may be ordered from the address below. From time to time other products - Address Books, Calendars, Table Mats, etc - are available.

The Internet

Already fifty thousand Frith photographs can be viewed and purchased on the internet through the Frith websites and a myriad of partner sites.

For more detailed information on Frith companies and products, look at these sites:

www.francisfrith.co.uk
www.francisfrith.com
(for North American visitors)

See the complete list of Frith Books at:
www.francisfrith.co.uk

This web site is regularly updated with the latest list of publications from the Frith Book Company. If you wish to buy books relating to another part of the country that your local bookshop does not stock, you may purchase on-line.

For further information, trade, or author enquiries please contact us at the address below:
The Francis Frith Collection, Frith's Barn, Teffont, Salisbury, Wiltshire, England SP3 5QP.
Tel: +44 (0)1722 716 376 Fax: +44 (0)1722 716 881 Email: sales@francisfrith.co.uk

See Frith books on the internet at www.francisfrith.co.uk

FREE MOUNTED PRINT

Mounted Print
Overall size 14 x 11 inches

Fill in and cut out this voucher and return *it with your remittance for £2.25 (to cover postage and handling). Offer valid for delivery to UK addresses only.*

Choose any photograph included in this book. *Your SEPIA print will be A4 in size. It will be mounted in a cream mount with a burgundy rule line (overall size 14 x 11 inches).*

Order additional Mounted Prints at HALF PRICE (only £7.49 each*)
If you would like to order more Frith prints from this book, possibly as gifts for friends and family, you can buy them at half price (with no additional postage and handling costs).

Have your Mounted Prints framed
For an extra £14.95 per print* you can have your mounted print(s) framed in an elegant polished wood and gilt moulding, overall size 16 x 13 inches (no additional postage and handling required).

*** IMPORTANT!**

These special prices are only available if you order at the same time as you order your free mounted print. You must use the ORIGINAL VOUCHER on this page (no copies permitted). We can only despatch to one address.

Send completed Voucher form to:
The Francis Frith Collection, Frith's Barn, Teffont, Salisbury, Wiltshire SP3 5QP

CHOOSE ANY IMAGE FROM THIS BOOK

Voucher *for **FREE** and Reduced Price Frith Prints*

Please do not photocopy this voucher. Only the original is valid, so please fill it in, cut it out and return it to us with your order.

Picture ref no	Page no	Qty	Mounted @ £7.49	Framed + £14.95	Total Cost
		1	Free of charge*	£	£
			£7.49	£	£
			£7.49	£	£
			£7.49	£	£
			£7.49	£	£
			£7.49	£	£
Please allow 28 days for delivery			* Post & handling (UK)		£2.25
			Total Order Cost		£

Title of this book ....

I enclose a cheque/postal order for £ ....
made payable to 'The Francis Frith Collection'

OR please debit my Mastercard / Visa / Switch / Amex card
(credit cards please on all overseas orders), details below

Card Number

Issue No (Switch only) Valid from (Amex/Switch)

Expires Signature

Name Mr/Mrs/Ms ....
Address ....
....
....
.... Postcode ....
Daytime Tel No ....
Email ....

Valid to 31/12/05

Free Print - see overleaf

Would you like to find out more about Francis Frith?

We have recently recruited some entertaining speakers who are happy to visit local groups, clubs and societies to give an illustrated talk documenting Frith's travels and photographs. If you are a member of such a group and are interested in hosting a presentation, we would love to hear from you.

Our speakers bring with them a small selection of our local town and county books, together with sample prints. They are happy to take orders. A small proportion of the order value is donated to the group who have hosted the presentation. The talks are therefore an excellent way of fundraising for small groups and societies.

Can you help us with information about any of the Frith photographs in this book?

We are gradually compiling an historical record for each of the photographs in the Frith archive. It is always fascinating to find out the names of the people shown in the pictures, as well as insights into the shops, buildings and other features depicted.

If you recognize anyone in the photographs in this book, or if you have information not already included in the author's caption, do let us know. We would love to hear from you, and will try to publish it in future books or articles.

Our production team

Frith books are produced by a small dedicated team at offices in the converted Grade II listed 18th-century barn at Teffont near Salisbury, illustrated above. Most have worked with the Frith Collection for many years. All have in common one quality: they have a passion for the Frith Collection. The team is constantly expanding, but currently includes:

Jason Buck, John Buck, Ruth Butler, Heather Crisp, David Davies, Isobel Hall, Julian Hight, Peter Horne, James Kinnear, Karen Kinnear, Tina Leary, Stuart Login, Amanda Lowe, David Marsh, Sue Molloy, Kate Rotondetto, Dean Scource, Eliza Sackett, Terence Sackett, Sandra Sampson, Adrian Sanders, Sandra Sanger, Julia Skinner, Claire Tarrier, Lewis Taylor, Shelley Tolcher and Lorraine Tuck.